# the **WHAM-O**®
# ULTIMATE
# FRISBEE®
## handbook

CIDER MILL
PRESS
BOOK
PUBLISHERS
kennebunkport, maine

D0005702

13 Digit ISBN: 978-1-60433-023-6
10 Digit ISBN: 1-60433-023-6

This book may be ordered by mail from the publisher. Please include $4.00 for postage and handling.
Please support your local bookseller first!

Books published by Cider Mill Press Book Publishers are available at special discounts for bulk purchases in the United States by corporations, institutions, and other organizations. For more information, please contact the publisher.

Applesauce Press is an imprint of Cider Mill Press Book Publishers "Where good books are ready for press"
12 Port Farm Road, Kennebunkport, Maine 04046

Visit us on the web! www.cidermillpress.com

Design by Jessica Disbrow Talley
Illustrations by Cynthia L. Copeland
Images courtesy of Phil Kennedy

Printed in China

2 3 4 5 6 7 8 9

# ACKNOWLEDGEMENTS

Thanks SO much to the following people for their enormous help in getting this handy guide off the ground and into your hands:

➤ David Waisblum of Wham-O®;

➤ Cynthia Hall Domine of Synchronicity;

➤ Sandy Hammerly, Executive Director, Ultimate Players Association;

➤ Arliss Paddock, copy editor;

➤ Jessica Disbrow Talley, designer;
   and

➤ Phil Kennedy of Wormhole Publishers, and his website www.FlatFlip.com,
   for giving us the skinny on the real history of the flying disc and kindly letting us
   reproduce some of his art.

Heads up!

# TABLE OF CONTENTS

# ULTIMATE:
## the essentials

There's no doubt you've seen people playing flying disc. Whether you live in the country, the suburbs, or a major city, just pass by any open field in the summertime, and you're likely to see a bunch of people—kids, adults, or a mix of both—throwing a disc around.

Chances are, at some point you might have seen a somewhat organized group of 14 or so people having a great time running, throwing, and vying for possession of a single disc. If so, you've probably seen a game of Ultimate in progress. (Originally called "Ultimate Frisbee®," after the amazingly popular flying-disc brand, now the sport is widely known as simply "Ultimate.") Or maybe you already know what a cool game this is, and you want to get in on the fun. If so, you'll find all you need right here to get together with your own friends and others for a competitive game of Ultimate.

Ultimate is played with two teams of seven. It's like a mix of football, basketball, and soccer, but it's played with a flying disc instead of a ball. It's an exciting game you can play throughout your life—all that it requires is that you're able to hustle up and down a grass-covered field with a bunch of your contemporaries. If you're mobile, give it a shot!

Ultimate is easy to learn, it's great exercise for the whole family, and it's essentially a non-contact sport. It makes for a great Thanksgiving Day interlude after the turkey and before the pumpkin pie. It's a player-defined, player-controlled team sport whose only referees are the players' sense of mutual respect and sportsmanship. Ultimate competitions include women's teams, men's teams, and mixed teams, and all levels of expertise can play, from novice to expert. Ultimate is fun to watch, fun to play, and takes little investment.

So dust off your disc—or better yet, buy yourself a brand-new one—and get ready for a good time!

# A LITTLE HISTORY

People have been throwing around disc-shaped objects for*ever*. The discus, tins, lids, plates … if it's flat and round and can fly through the air, it's fair game, right? But it was the enterprising Fred Morrison who came up with the idea for selling flying discs after he started tossing around a popcorn-can lid in 1937 with his girl, Lucille, at a Thanksgiving Day bash in Los Angeles. That popcorn lid led to cake pans, and eventually, after flying fighter bombers in WWII, Fred designed a disc he named the Whirlo-Way. He teamed up with Warren Franscioni (the guy with the dough) to mold hard plastic discs based on his design.

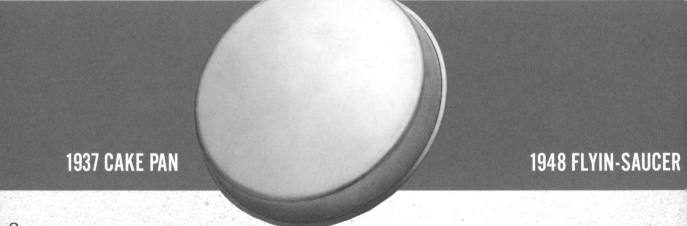

1937 CAKE PAN

1948 FLYIN-SAUCER

Around this time UFOs were being reported as flying-saucer sightings so Fred and Warren changed the name to the "Flyin-Saucer." The business shut down a few years later, but Fred wasn't done yet! In 1955 he started producing his own discs in a new design he called the Pluto Platter. Wham-O® perked up its enterprising ears and in 1957 took over.

Meanwhile, at Yale University, college students were tossing around the empty pie tins from the nearby Frisbie Pie Company. They started yelling out "Frisbie!" as a heads-up. Soon Wham-O® was selling the Pluto Platters to these kids who nicknamed them "Frisbies." Wham-O® loved the nickname and jumped on board, trademarked the name and changed the spelling to Frisbee®.

1957 PLUTO PLATTER

Some people have called it Ultimate Frisbee®, others have called it Frisbee® Football, but now it's widely known as simply Ultimate—and it is the ultimate!

Want to know more? Check out Phil Kennedy's site www.FlatFlip.com and the book he wrote with Fred Morrison called *Flat Flip Flies Straight, True Origins of the Frisbee*®. You'll be the resident flying disc genius!

# FUN FACTS

Here are some fun facts about this awesome game:

➡ Ultimate is self-governing—which means no referees!

➡ The object of the game is to catch a throw in your opponent's end zone.

➡ Most games are played until one team has 15 points, with a 2-point spread necessary to win.

➡ If you're holding the disc, you can't run. (This was not one of the original rules, but was added later.)

➡ The original rules allowed for as many as 30 players.

➡ Ultimate rules can be changed to suit the players, as long as everyone agrees. So even the field size can change!

➡ Two fun variants of the game are Beach Ultimate and Indoor Ultimate. (Check the resources section at the back of the book for where you can learn more about these.)

➡ Research shows that each year, more flying discs are sold worldwide than footballs, baseballs, and basketballs combined!

> "Ultimate Frisbee® combines speed, grace, and powerful hurling with a grueling pace."
> — *The Wall Street Journal*

# WHAT YOU'LL NEED

You don't get to play many sports that require such little maintenance or equipment. Ultimate is light on the "stuff," which makes it very attractive to students on a budget or people on the move. All you'll need to play a game of Ultimate is:

- 2 teams of 7 people each
- 8 cones to mark the end zones
- a flying disc (if you're playing in a tournament, a 175-gram disc is used, and must be approved by both teams)
- chalk (optional)

# THE PLAYING FIELD

Ultimate can be played on any field, but the more smooth and level it is, the better. Clear the field of debris, and mark the boundaries with chalk if you have some. (You can use other types of marker as well—anything that won't be a hazard or damage the grass or the field.)

The standard field is 120 yards long, including two 25-yard end zones. The width is 40 yards. Use the cones to mark off the corners of the end zones. In other words, the area not including the end zones is 70 yards long by 40 yards wide. (This is the middle of the field.) Mark this accordingly. Then add on 25-yard by 40-yard end zones to each end. Place the cones at the corners of the end zone.

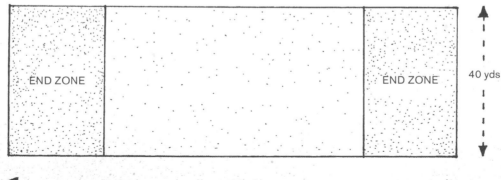

# GETTING READY

After you've set up the playing field, there's not much else you have to do to get ready to play Ultimate. But stretching before you start playing is highly recommended. As with any physical activity, limbering-up beforehand can help to prevent any kind of injury. Try the following stretches, which will only take a few minutes:

## Stretch #1:

Stretch your arms straight up above your head, and reach for the ceiling. Then lower them to the floor in front of you as you bend from the waist. Touch the floor with your hands (if you can touch the floor—just go as far as is reasonably comfortable). Try to stretch from your lower back instead of from your hamstrings. Hang there for 10 or 20 seconds, and then bend your knees and slowly come back up. Repeat two more times.

If you can't reach all the way to the floor, hang from the waist and grab your elbows with the opposite hands. Let the weight of your body pull you down toward the floor as you gently swing back and forth, from side to side.

## Stretch #2

Face a wall and lean your hands on it, palms down, while moving your feet farther away from the wall so that your body is at an incline. Stretch your hamstrings by moving up on the ball of one foot, and then the other. Heel, toe … heel, toe. Repeat on each side five times.

## Stretch #3

Another great stretch that will really limber you up is to do leg lunges. Stand up straight, with your hands on your hips. Reach your left leg out as far as you can in front of you, and move forward and down so that your left leg bends at the knee at a 90-degree angle. Keep your heels on the floor if you can. Come back up and switch legs. Do five lunges on each side.

There are plenty of other things you can do beforehand that will help you to limber up (like jogging for a few minutes, doing jumping-jacks, etc.), but the thing to know is that it's important to warm up properly before you start a full game of running around the field—and throwing, catching, cutting, and marking. (Don't worry, we'll get to all that!)

Whenever you start a new sport, it's important to be patient with yourself. You will master the moves of Ultimate in time, and with luck you'll soon be an Ultimate wizard. But the rules of mastery are practice, practice, practice. You can do drills with your team members to work on your moves with them. You can also practice in your yard with a disc by yourself. Just be prepared to run back and forth a lot to retrieve the disc. (Or better yet, train the dog!)

# THE SPIRIT OF THE GAME

One thing that sets Ultimate apart from most other sports is that players are responsible for their own plays and calls. There are no referees! The spirit of great sportsmanship is alive and well on the Ultimate playing field. Any game of Ultimate is self-officiating—from the backyard, to the world championships. And believe it or not, it works.

Ultimate calls for great respect for the game and for your fellow players. This tradition of respect and sportsmanship holds the game together, and is of paramount importance as its governing principle. There is no name-calling, intentional fouling, or aggression on the Ultimate field. Each player respects himself and his team. The "Spirit of the Game" makes Ultimate an attractive sport for many people who don't usually like competitive sports.

At the beginner's level, a new player can expect to be treated with respect as she learns the rules, helps others to learn along with her and, in turn, eventually teaches others. At more advanced levels, players exhibit great respect for the rules and take responsibility for knowing all the rules.

As the sport is self-governing, it's important that each team-member commit the rules to heart as soon as possible. Remember, if someone fouls, it might be up to you to call it! We'll get into how to settle disputes later on, but overall you should know that Ultimate is quite the gentleman's (and gentlewoman's) sport.

But don't be fooled by all this knightly behavior: Ultimate is still a very competitive sport!

# THROWING TECHNIQUES:
## basic moves

Before we get into how to actually play Ultimate (and we will—don't worry!), let's first get into how to throw the disc.

## EASY SNEEZY: THE BACKHAND

Chances are you've already thrown a flying disc around at some time in your life. If you have, this is probably the throw you used. In Ultimate, this is probably the easiest, most basic throw. Picture yourself hitting a backhand in tennis: this is the basic movement of the backhand disc-throw. Grab a disc (and a friend, if you have one handy—if not, grab your mom) and head outside. (It's really not a good idea to practice disc-throwing inside.)

Give yourself some room to throw the disc. Hold the disc in whichever hand is more comfortable for you. If the disc is in your right hand, align yourself so that you're standing sideways in relation to the person you're going to throw to, with feet shoulder-width apart and your right shoulder pointing toward the person. (If it's in your left hand, vice versa.)

Place your thumb on the top side of the disc, and curl your other fingers under the disc, almost like you are making a fist. Hold the disc parallel to the ground. You will step with the foot that is on the same side of the body as your throwing hand. So if you are a righty, ready to throw with your right hand, you're going to step out with your right foot as you throw. (Before you throw, your weight should be back, on your left leg.)

Keep your eye on the person receiving the throw (the receiver), and shift your weight forward. Swing your arm back across your body, then straight out toward the receiver in a smooth motion, and release the disc flat. To help you keep the disc parallel to the ground, pretend that you're balancing something on top of it. Snap your wrist to put some spin into your throw, swing your arm out in a smooth motion, and release the disc in that position. Follow through with your body, moving in the same direction as your throw.

Practice this throw until you feel you've gained some mastery. It's a basic move you will be using over and over in a game of Ultimate. See if you can throw a backhand so that your receiver doesn't have to run to catch it. Once you've mastered this throw, move on to the forehand throw.

When throwing a disc, it's important to snap your wrist to get momentum—you'll need to get enough force behind the throw to give it some distance.

# THE FOREHAND

The forehand throw is another necessary, basic move you'll be using frequently in the game of Ultimate. The grip is different from that used in the backhand.

For this throw, your middle finger and index finger should be held together, with your middle finger pressing against the inside rim of the disc. If this feels too difficult, you can stretch out your index finger for more support and control, but doing so will sacrifice some force and momentum.

Place your ring finger and pinky finger on the outside rim of the disc, with the ring finger exerting pressure toward the top side of the disc for added stability. The thumb is on the top of the disc with the nail facing upward. Your palm should be pointing up toward the sky. Stand with your legs shoulder-width apart.

If this feels awkward at first, don't worry. Soon it will be second nature as you master the basic moves of Ultimate.

Now get ready to release the disc. Once again, align your body toward your receiver. Step out with the foot that is on the same side of your body and your throwing hand. So if you are throwing with your left hand, step out with your left foot. Keep the palm of your throwing hand facing upward, and once again try to release the disc flat and level. Again, picture yourself balancing something on top of the disc to keep it level. Snap your wrist to gain momentum, and let it fly!

Practice your forehand over and over again with an Ultimate buddy until you are very comfortable with it. This throw might take a little longer to master than the backhand, but keep at it. Remember, practice is the only way to get there!

# THE HAMMER

Now you're ready for a more advanced move. The Hammer is an overhead throw that begins with the forehand grip, then the disc is released at an angle so that it flattens out and flies upside down.
As always, keep an eye on the receiver. A common beginner error is to keep your eye on the disc instead of on your target.

Have your weight on your non-pivot foot—that is, on your foot that's on the same side as your throwing hand. (Your pivot foot is the foot opposite your throwing hand.)

You are going to cock the disc beside your head and bring the disc forward, shifting your weight to your other foot as you do so. You should gain some momentum by doing this. Release the disc in front of you and above your head. For this throw you don't want the disc to be level; you are going to release it at a 45-degree angle. Think of a football pass: this is the movement you are trying to mimic.

## A throw can go in any direction: forward, backward, whatever!

For maximum effect with the hammer, put as much spin as possible on the disc. This means snapping your wrist expertly, so make sure you are practicing your wrist-snaps with your other throws. As you release the disc, you should notice that it flies in an arc toward the receiver. It quickly settles into a flat position as it soars, but the disc will be flying upside down.

## Adjust the angle of your releases to play with the direction of your hammer throw. As you adjust, you'll see what works and what doesn't. You'll be able to fine-tune your throw until others will wonder how you got to be such an amazing Ultimate thrower!

Don't beat yourself up if this one is hard to master. The hammer is an advanced move and will take some practice to perfect. It's a good show-off move when you want to impress someone. But only, of course, if you can do it right. So get out there and start throwing!

# OUTSIDE-IN RELEASES AND INSIDE-OUT RELEASES

The angle at which the disc ends up flying through the air is referred to as an Outside-In release or an Inside-Out release. This angle affects the arc the disc will fly in, ultimately affecting where the disc will end up.

    If you release the disc so that it flies with the outside edge tilted up (as opposed to flying level), it's an Outside-In release. But if you release the disc with the outside edge tilted down, it's called an Inside-Out release. Know your terminology to become the expert you aspire to be!

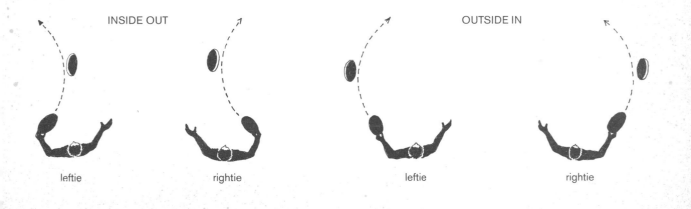

INSIDE OUT                 OUTSIDE IN

leftie        rightie            leftie        rightie

If you are a total geek and need to know exactly how the disc works aerodynamically, you can check out a site all about "Frisbee® Physics," as explained on the PBS show "Newton's Apple," at http://www.mansfieldct.org/schools/MMS/staff/hand/Flightfrisbee.htm.

# THE HAWK

Here's one more throw for you to learn that's very useful in Ultimate. A Hawk is a throw that goes very long: it arcs across the field, soaring in the air toward the receiver. It's one of the game's most exciting throws, and you'll want to practice long throws so you can master the game.

Hawks are in the air longer than other throws, so the chances of someone intercepting the receiver are pretty good. So you'll want to make sure the receiver is wide open before you throw a Hawk in his or her direction. You don't want to give defense a lot of time to catch up!

Because Hawks cover so much ground, they can be difficult to throw accurately. But there's nothing quite as impressive as seeing a disc flying across a field only to land expertly in a receiver's waiting hands!

# CATCHING TECHNIQUES

Now that you are an ace at throwing, you'll want to give your poor Ultimate training partner a break and switch. It's time to learn how to catch! You may ask yourself what the big deal is about catching. After all, you can catch a football or a baseball with no problem. But there are specific catches you need to be aware on in order to maximize efficiency on the field.

## LAYING OUT

Everyone wants to try laying out when they start playing Ultimate. It's the coolest move around! Laying out is when you dive for the disc in order to catch it.

You need to practice your dives before you, well, dive in—otherwise you might get hurt.

Before you lay out, you'll want to make sure the ground is safe to dive on. If you're in a park where there might be glass and other dangerous debris, skip laying out and let the disc go. It's just not worth it.

But if you go for it, do this: drop to your knees and stretch out your arms as far as possible. Make sure you land on your hips and stomach so you have some padding under yourself to cushion your fall. Landing on joints can be painful, and you risk injury.

Practice laying out in a safe (embarrassment-free) environment, then go impress your friends!

# THE CLAP

The Clap, also known as the Pancake Catch, is easy to master. It's the no-fail way to catch, and should be your default catch for straight-on throws when the disc lands in the area between your waist and your head. If the throw is not straight on, you may need to slide or adjust your position in order to catch it, but in a slide it's still easier to catch with the clap than any other way.

To catch with the Clap, simply get your body in front of the disc, hands and feet apart. Spread your fingers so you have more ground you can cover with the catch. When the disc flies toward you, just clap your hands together from top to bottom and secure the disc tightly. *Voilà!* One successful catch has been mastered.

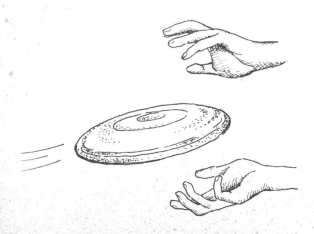

# TWO-HANDED RIM CATCH

If there's no way a Clap Catch is going to make it, you can try for a Two-Handed Rim Catch. This catch is optimally made when the disc is above your shoulders or below your hips. Thumb positioning is important here: If the disc is above your shoulders, make sure your thumb is beneath the disc when you catch it. If the disc is below your hips, make sure your thumb is on top of the disc. This is a harder catch than the Clap, so you risk dropping the disc. Practice before taking this move in a game when it really matters.

## CATCHING TIP

Whatever you do, don't take your eyes off the disc. You want to watch it until you catch it. Then turn your attention back to the field. If you take your eyes off the disc to plan your next move, chances are you'll drop it.

# ONE-HANDED RIM CATCH

Another option for catching is the One-Handed Rim Catch, which (as you probably guessed, genius!) is harder than the Two-Handed Rim Catch. Only use this move when the throw is way low, way high, way out in back of you, or nearly out of reach in front of you. It's a very risky move that should only be attempted when the Two-Handed just won't cut it. The same thumb positioning applies here as it does with the Two-Handed, so follow the directions above.

If a defensive player and an offensive player catch a disc at the same time, the disc goes to the offense.

# THE IMPORTANCE OF PRACTICE

You are sick and tired of practicing. All anyone tells you is to practice, practice, practice. But you just want to get out there and play. Well, think of it this way: you may be the best runner, the best thrower, the best-looking person on the team. But if you can't catch a throw, no one will be throwing to you, and you'll be, in effect, left out of the game. Don't let this happen to you. Practice!

# ON THE OFFENSIVE

Before we go over the rules of the game, let's review the strategies you'll want to know so you can beat the pants off your opponents. First, let's review the offensive strategies that are absolutely necessary for a competitive game of Ultimate.

# CUTTING

The basic rule of the game is to get your disc down the field so someone can catch in the end zone and score for your team. So what's so hard about that, you might ask? Well, the whole time your team is trying to move the disc down the field, your opponents are trying to stop you. In other words, the whole time you'll be covered by a defensive player who is doing her best to distract you and prevent you from making a successful catch.

In order to get away from the defensive player who is stuck to you like glue, you'll want to master the art of cutting. Cutting is moving toward the receiver by suddenly changing direction, or veering off unexpectedly so that the defense doesn't know what's happening.

If you can't get away from the defensive player by running in one direction, try to fake her out, and make your move when he goes in the wrong direction. Get your defensive player off-balance by cutting or faking him out and running in the opposite direction. If you're not sure how this is done, just watch some squirrels or rabbits. They are masters of cutting! You must really run all-out in order to beat your opponent. If you're slow, you'll never get away.

# TIPS FOR BECOMING A CUTTING ACE

Here are a few cutting tips:

➡ Always keep your eye on the thrower. You may be busy cutting across the field, wide open for a throw, but you are so busy cutting away you forget to watch the thrower. You'll never make a catch this way. So always pay attention to what the thrower is doing: she may be waiting for eye contact from you!

➡ Make sure you are cutting to the open side of the field. There's no point in cutting away and finding yourself blocked from making a good catch by too many players crowding the field.

➡ Make sure your cuts are sharp. Don't arc into it—you want something more dramatic.

➡ The most important part of a cut is changing direction.

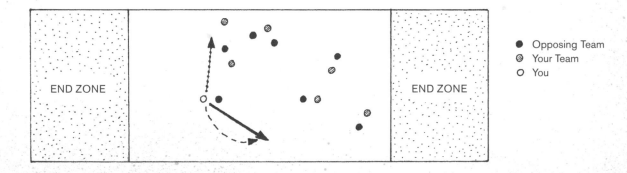

END ZONE

END ZONE

● Opposing Team
◍ Your Team
○ You

# STRATEGY: THE STACK

One awesome basic strategy for offensive players is called the Stack. The Stack allows your team to create space on the field for receivers to cut into. To create a Stack, have all team players spaced out in a line up the middle of the field. Each player in the Stack will be 3 to 5 yards away from the next player. The wide-open spaces on either side of the Stack are used for cutting, while the Stack itself is known as the "dead zone."

If a player makes a successful cut, he should then fold back into the Stack and allow the next player to make a cut into the open space or "cutting zone."

A Stack gives some order to the field, and allows for players to leave themselves open for a successful pass.

The thrower will be about 10 yards away from the first member of the Stack. Ideally, Stack members who are farther away, closer to the end zone, will hopefully try to break free and clear of defense, leaving themselves open for a catch. Once the disc has been caught, this player will throw again to someone else breaking free of the Stack, until a player makes it to the end zone and positions himself for a successful catch.

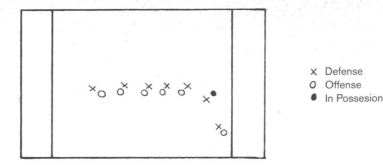

x   Defense
o   Offense
●   In Possesion

A Stack gives structure to the offense and provides an efficient means of moving the disc down the field. Try drills with your team to master the Stack. Make sure you practice the Stack on both backhand and forehand sides. You want to be prepared for the big game!

For a fun twist, try the Stack with a Hawk thrown in. See how long you can go!

For a great reference on other offense strategies, see The Ultimate Handbook website, at www.ultimatehandbook.com.

For a successful catch, don't stop and wait until the disc lands in your arms. Run toward the disc to protect yourself from a defense interception.

# DEFENSIVE MOVES

You will also need to learn how to be a great defensive player if you want to be an Ultimate champ.

## MARKING

Marking is the basic defense skill of trying to limit the number of throws a thrower can make. As a marker, you are basically trying to make it as hard as possible for the thrower to throw the disc. If you are the marker, you will get into position in front of the thrower and start to distract the thrower from making a successful throw. You can do this by shuffling your feet back and forth and waving your arms around in a distracting manner.

But never forget the Spirit of the Game, so essential to Ultimate. You may NOT shout obscenities about the other player's mother, touch the other player, or be rude and aggressive in any way. If you do so, you don't belong on the Ultimate field, where respect is central to the game.

In order to maintain good balance, keep your legs shoulder-width apart and your knees flexible. You'll be sturdy and ready for action if necessary. Remember, the thrower will try to fake you out, so you want to be alert and ready for anything. Try to "read" the thrower.

## A marker should stay at least a foot away from the thrower at all times.

The thrower is only allowed to hold the disc for 10 seconds. It's your job as marker to count off the time. This is called the Stall Count. Start by saying "Stall One," and continue to "Stall Nine," at one-second intervals. When the disc is released, it's the marker's job to call out "Up!" This signals to your team members that the disc is airborne.

If the marker calls "Stall Ten," it's a turnover. (For more on turnovers, see the chapter on Violations.)

## A marker isn't trying to stop the offense from throwing, but trying to limit the number of throws the offense makes.

# STRATEGY: MAY THE FORCE BE WITH YOU

One defense strategy is the Force. In the Force, the marker is putting the squeeze on the thrower and forcing the thrower to throw on one side only. In other words, the marker is limiting the thrower's choices.

The team strategy comes into play as the defense team members recognize the Force in action, and move into position to prevent the receiver from successfully completing the throw. In other words, they move into position to block the open sections of the field that the receiver will try to position. In a forced forehand, the Marker forces the thrower to throw to the forehand side of the field. In a forced backhand, the Marker forces the thrower to throw to the backhand side of the field. Remember, the backhand is like a tennis backhand, so if you're a righty the throw will go to the right, and vice versa.

Practice your marking, Stall Counting, and Forces before moving on to the Downfield Defending skills.

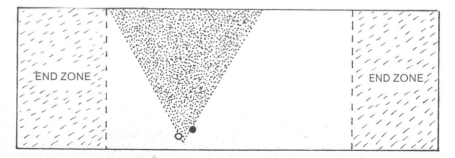

END ZONE          END ZONE

● Defender
O Thrower

# STRATEGY: DOWNFIELD DEFENDING

Now that you've mastered some basic defense skills you can use with the thrower, you'll want to master the downfield defender skills. The part of the downfield defender is to stop the player he's covering from getting the disc downfield.

You must pay careful attention if you are playing the part of the downfield defender. You want to know if the Force taking place upfield is a forced backhand or forced forehand, so that you'll know which way the throw is going. If you can predict this, you'll know which way the receiver is going to head to try to catch the disc.

Again, you want to stay balanced by keeping your knees flexible and your legs shoulder-width apart. You want to be able to react at a second's notice to the movements of the receiver.

In order to be a champion defender you have to watch the field at all times. Know what's going on near you, but also all the way across the field.

# FANCY FEET

A key basic move in Ultimate is the pivot. Practice your pivots regularly so you can fake effectively and throw more easily. Your pivot foot is always the foot opposite your throwing hand. This foot must remain in the same spot when you have the disc. If the foot slides or comes off the ground, you risk a violation (see the chapter on Violations). While pivoting, stay balanced so you can move easily back and forth if necessary. Practice pivots by faking out your opponent. Fakes and pivots are essential moves for both offense and defense.

# FOULS & VIOLATIONS

There are certain violations and fouls in Ultimate. First, we'll cover the fouls.

## FOULS

A foul occurs when there is physical contact between players. If there is contact in the game that affects the outcome of a play, a foul is called. The only player who can call the foul is the player who has been fouled. A player who wants to call a foul must yell out, "Foul!", and play stops.

## THE CHECK

When play stops, all players must stop where they are, doing their best to retain their positions. Whoever has possession of the disc keeps the disc.

Play doesn't restart until the marker touches the thrower's disc. If the disc is thrown before this formality, the disc is returned to the thrower, who must start again.

A foul is on the player who initiates the contact. Remember, this is a gentleman's game; in the case of a foul, the two team members involved discuss the foul and try to come to an agreement. If the player who is called for the foul agrees that he fouled the other player, the fouled player takes possession of the disc. Any discussion is undertaken with great respect for each other. If players cannot resolve a dispute, the disc is returned to the thrower, and play resumes.

If a thrower is fouled while throwing and the receiver catches the throw, the play continues. If the player is fouled while throwing and the disc is not caught, the disc is returned to the thrower. If the marker is fouled during a throw and the play is not received, the game continues.

If bodily contact occurs after the thrower has released the disc, no foul is called. However, physical contact should be avoided as much as possible.

Fouls can also be committed during catches. If a player interferes with a catch, a foul is called. If the person who fouls the catcher agrees with the foul, the catcher retains possession of the disc. If the foul is disputed, the disc is returned to the thrower. It should be noted that any physical contact is frowned upon, though some is undeniably unavoidable. However, any intentional rough-housing or reckless or aggressive behavior will resolve in a foul against the aggressor. Remember the Spirit of the Game! If you want a rough-and-tumble game, go play football.

# VIOLATIONS

Violations are instances where the rules are broken or disregarded without physical contact taking place. For example, traveling is considered a violation in Ultimate.

Traveling, as described earlier, occurs when a thrower's pivot foot slides on the ground or leaves the ground completely. Traveling also occurs when a receiver catches a throw and continues to move, even though it's obvious the movement is overkill and completely unnecessary. (Watch out for drama queens who will try to overemphasize a catch to sneak farther down the field. Devious!)

So what happens when a travel is called? Play immediately stops for a check.

You can also cause a violation by stripping. A strip is when a player on defense touches a thrower or a receiver. If you are the thrower or receiver and a defensive player touches you, you should call out "Strip!", retake possession of the disc, and continue playing.

Occasionally, a strip will occur during a Stall Count. If this happens, the player in possession at the time of the violation retakes the disc, and the marker resumes the count from one—"Stall One!"

Don't you just love a sport with its own vocabulary? So cool.

A pick is another type of violation of the rules. A pick occurs when an offensive player moves to obstruct the play of a member on the defensive team. If a pick is called, a check goes into effect.

Only one marker may guard a thrower. If more than one player attempts to guard a thrower, a violation occurs. If this happens, a player will call out, "Double Team!", and two counts must be subtracted from the marker's Stall Count. Play fair: No double teaming!"

# READY, SET, PLAY!

Now that you've gotten all the moves and strategies down, it's time to play a game of Ultimate. Get your team members together, and lay out the boundaries of the field.

Ready? OK, let's go. The game is started by a pull. A pull is the first throw of the game. One team throws the disc down the field to the other team and initiates play. This is not a scoring throw, it's just the initiating throw.

The pulling team must stay in their end zone until the disc is thrown. The receiving team members must all have at least one foot on the goal line of their side of the field. Once the disc is released, all players can move across the field. The pulling team cannot touch the disc until it has been touched by the opposing team. If no one catches the disc, play resumes where the disc fell. If the disc goes out of bounds and no one catches it, it's called a "brick."

The disc is put back into play nearest to where it went out of bounds, or on the spot in the middle of the field closest to where it went out of bounds. Or, you can start over. If the receiving team catches the disc, then drops it, a "turnover" is called. A turnover is a change in possession of the disc. In other words, the other team now gets the disc.

Most Ultimate games have a halftime. A pull starts the game off again after halftime.

# TURNOVERS

Here is your handy turnover list. A turnover takes place when any of the following occur:

➡ The stall count reaches Stall 10.

➡ A throw is intercepted.

➡ A throw is incomplete. (Incomplete passes included fumbles by the thrower that involve no defensive interference.)

➡ A throw is out of bounds.

➡ A disc is handed to another player instead of thrown.

➡ The thrower catches their own throw.

# OBJECTIVES

Each team is trying to get a player into the end zone who can catch the disc while there. Remember, a player cannot run into the end zone with the disc. The game play is all about using the team members to move the disc down the field.

Each end-zone catch is worth one point. The team with 15 points (with a 2-point spread) wins! Ultimate is a flexible game, however. Anything can change, as long as both teams agree: you can change the dimensions of the field, the number of players, the number of points needed to win ... it's your game!

If a point is scored, the team that scored then pulls to the other team to restart play.

# SET YOUR BOUNDARIES

Anywhere on the playing field is considered in-bounds, except for the field lines. If a player catches a disc while on the perimeter lines, she's out of bounds. In other words, the perimeter lines are out of bounds.

# CLUBS & ORGANIZATIONS

So now you've played Ultimate, and you're wondering how you can connect with others who share your love and respect of the game. Well, you're in luck. This is an organized sport that goes all the way up to World Championships. So keep practicing: You never know if you might end up in the Ultimate Hall of Fame someday!

# THE ULTIMATE PLAYERS ASSOCIATION

Founded in 1979 and based in Boulder, Colorado, the Ultimate Players Association acts as the sport's governing body in the U.S. It's among the first flying-disc sport organizations in the world, and one of the largest, with more than 27,300 members. The UPA has named a national champion every year since 1979. UPA is a player-run, not-for-profit organization whose mission is "to advance the sport of Ultimate in the United States by enhancing and promoting Character, Community, and Competition." Check out the UPA website (http://www.upa.org) for in-depth explanation of the rules, and for the more subtle rule-calls you'll have to make. As you play, questions will come up, and the UPA website can most certainly answer them for you. It's a terrific resource that shouldn't be overlooked. Whether you'd like to compete or simply watch at an official game, on the site you'll also find a listing of upcoming tournaments.

# THE WORLD FLYING DISC FEDERATION

You'll also want to check out the website for the World Flying Disc Federation (http://www.wfdf.org). With member associations in 46 countries, WFDF is a coalition of the national organizations that govern their respective flying-disc sports—which include Disc Golf, Freestyle, Guts, DDC, and Field Events, as well as Ultimate. WFDF hosts the World Championships, and develops the rules of the game.

# STATE, REGIONAL, AND LOCAL GROUPS

There are also more local Ultimate organizations—such as the Boston Ultimate Disc Association, in Massachusetts, and Westchester Ultimate Disc, in New York—so search the UPA site and elsewhere online for groups near you. Colleges, high schools, and even middle schools are now hosting Ultimate teams. If you search, you shall find.

Have fun! UP!

# LINGO:
## your ultimate glossary

## BACKHAND
A simple throw.

## BRICK
A pull that goes out of bounds without being caught.

## CHECK
When play stops, all players must stop where they are, doing their best to retain their positions.

## CLAP (or Pancake) CATCH
A catch made by clapping two hands together from above and below.

## CUTTING
An offensive move, where a player cuts away from the defense in order to break free.

## CUTTING ZONE
The clear spaces on either side of a stack.

## DEAD ZONE
A Stack is also known as the Dead Zone.

## DOUBLE-TEAM
When more than one player attempts to guard a thrower.

## FOREHAND
A throw that is somewhat harder to master than the backhand.

## FOUL
Caused by physical contact between players.

## HAMMER
A sophisticated throw that builds on the forehand. Hard to master.

## HAWK
A long throw. Leaves you open for defense to catch up.

## LAYING OUT
Diving for the disc in order to catch it.

## ONE-HANDED RIM CATCH
A difficult catch to be used for very high throws or very low throws. Also used when the disc is way out in front of you or way out behind you. Very hard to master.

## PICK
When an offensive player moves to obstruct the play of a member on the defensive team.

## PIVOT FOOT
The foot on the opposite side from the throwing hand. Must not leave the ground during a throw. (See "Travel.")

## PULL
The throw that starts the game, either at the beginning or after halftime. It's not considered a throw for scoring.

## SPIRIT OF THE GAME

Ultimate is a self-governing game and each player takes responsibility for the rules. Spirit of the Game is the spirit of responsibility and respect that runs through the sport of Ultimate, from novice to champion.

## STACK

An offensive move, wherein the players line up in the middle of the field to create Cutting Zones on either side of the Stack, allowing spaces for players to cut through.

## STRIP

When a player on defense touches a thrower or a receiver.

## TRAVEL

When a thrower picks up or slides his pivot foot while throwing or pivoting. A violation.

## TWO-HANDED RIM CATCH

A catch made when the disc is above your shoulders or below your hips; harder catch than the Clap.

## ULTIMATE

The coolest game in the world!

# WEBSITES & RESOURCES

## THE ULTIMATE PLAYERS' ASSOCIATION

http://www.upa.org

The Ultimate Players' Association was founded in 1979. It is among the first flying-disc sport organizations in the world, and one of the largest, with over 24,600 members and hundreds of volunteers. It was also a wonderful resource for this book. (Thanks, UPA!)

# THE WORLD FLYING DISC FEDERATION

http://www.wfdf.org

The World Flying Disc Federation (WFDF) is made up of the national organizations and federations that govern their respective disc sports (such as Ultimate, Disc Golf, Freestyle, and more). WFDF is host of the World Championships.

# THE ULTIMATE HANDBOOK

http://www.ultimatehandbook.com/uh/home.html

This comprehensive site for Ultimate players of all levels provides information that will help you develop core skills, perfect strategies, and catch up on news of the Ultimate community.

# FRISBEEDISC.COM

http://www.frisbeedisc.com/sports/ultimate

Head to this site for game tips and information on Ultimate Frisbee® products, and learn about the Youth Outreach kit that has all you need to get Ultimate Frisbee® started in your school's physical education program. Also check out the site of the Wham-O® company, **www.wham-o.com**, to learn about the sport's history, shop online for Frisbee® Disc products, and more.

## BEACH ULTIMATE LOVERS ASSOCIATION

http://beachultimate.org

The Beach Ultimate Lovers Association (BULA) is the international governing body for Beach Ultimate, a fun variant of the game played on sand, with smaller teams. On the site you'll find lots of info, including worldwide listings of where you can watch or play Beach Ultimate. (Hey, this would be great to do while you're on vacation!)

## EXPERT VILLAGE

http://www.expertvillage.com

This site is a great source of how-to videos on a lot of topics. Just type "Ultimate" in the search bar at the top of the page, and you'll have access to a number of really helpful videos that show Ultimate play and techniques.

## UK INDOOR ULTIMATE RULES

http://www.ukultimate.com/system/files/ukua+indoor+ultimate+rules+2007.pdf

In northern climes and in the wintertime, Ultimate is often played indoors. Here you'll find official WFDF rules for playing indoors as played in the United Kingdom.

# THE AUSTRALIA FLYING DISC ASSOCIATION

http://www.afda.com

The AFDA is the go-to organization in Australia for all things Ultimate Down Under. Check out this site for news about tournaments, skills clinics, coaching, and more.

# NEW ZEALAND ULTIMATE

http://www.ultimate.org.nz

With its mission statement "to direct and develop Ultimate in New Zealand," this is a wonderful resource for info on NZ-related Ultimate tournaments, rules, awards, and links.

# WHAT IS ULTIMATE?

http://www.whatisultimate.com

A fun site about Ultimate, it includes the Ultimate Archive, a collection of articles about the sport published in different media from around the world.

## ABOUT CIDER MILL PRESS

Good ideas ripen with time. From seed to harvest, Cider Mill Press strives to bring fine reading, information, and entertainment together between the covers of its creatively crafted books. Our Cider Mill bears fruit twice a year, publishing a new crop of titles each spring and fall.

## VISIT US ON THE WEB AT

www.cidermillpress.com
or write to us at
12 Port Farm Road
Kennebunkport, Maine 04046